LIKE I GIVE A FROCK

LiKe I give a frock

fashion forecasts
and meaningless
misguidance

BY MICHI GIRL XX

CHRONICLE BOOKS
SAN FRANCISCO

First published in the United States of America in 2009
by Chronicle Books LLC.

First published by Penguin Group (Australia) in 2008.

Text copyright © 2008 by Chloe Quigley and Daniel
Pollock. Illustrations copyright © 2008 by Kat Macleod.
All rights reserved. No part of this book may be
reproduced in any form without written permission
from the publisher.

Library of Congress Cataloging-in-Publication
Data available.

ISBN: 978-0-8118-6888-4

Cover and text design by Simone Elder, Ortolan
Illustrations by Kat Macleod, Ortolan
Manufactured in China

10 9 8 7 6 5 4 3 2 1

Chronicle Books LLC
680 Second Street
San Francisco, California 94107

www.chroniclebooks.com

CONTENTS

DEDICATED
TO ME

The odds of being struck by lightening are approximately 1 in 800,000.

• CALL SHRINK ABOUT HEIGHTENED SENSE OF AWARENESS AND RESTLESSNESS - HAVE OVERWHELMING SPRING FEVER - FEEL I MIGHT START SEEING DEAD PEOPLE SOON. IS IT POSSIBLE TO BE SO IN TUNE WITH THE UNIVERSE?

• NOTE: IF I WERE SO IN TUNE WITH ENTIRE UNIVERSE PERHAPS I COULD SENSE LOST AND LONELY MARNI DRESSES AT FAR AWAY OP SHOPS IN NEED OF RESCUING? INVESTIGATE NEW SIXTH SENSE.

• MY LIFE AS GIRL ABOUT TOWN IS OFFICIALLY A CLICHÉ. IT'S SPRING AND NOT ONLY DO I HAVE THE URGE IN THE BEDROOM (IF YOU KNOW WHAT I MEAN), I HAVE THE URGE TO CLEAN OUT MY CUPBOARDS TOO.

In enormous show of restraint, put new season Viktor & Rolf dress on layby, intention being I would pay it off in time for Christmas parties. In enormous show of greed collected dress following lunchtime. Always did think layby was the fashion equivalent of masochism.

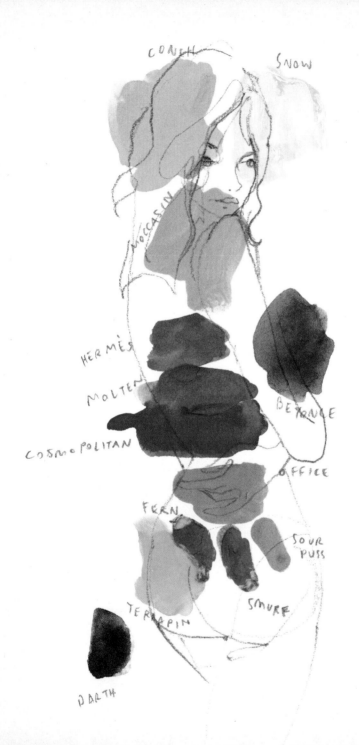

COLOR ME BAD

Every season it happens to all
of them. Like an aging spinster,
the humble color goes through
a mid-life crisis and thinks
it has to reinvent itself in
order to become more attractive.

Gray becomes moccasin.
White becomes snow.
Beige becomes conch.
And green goes to fern,
naturally.

Right now there's probably
some six-year-old in the
suburbs whining to the teacher
because she's all out of
Hermès fingerpaint.

THERE'S NO SUCH THING AS THE 'NEW BLACK'
— DARTH VADER

You can say what you like about
fashion — it's frivolous,
indulgent, fun — but it can also
be downright evil. Take the
jumpsuit, for instance. Is the
distance from shoulders to possum
standard across all women?
I think not. One girl's comfort
zone is another's camel toe.
So when faced with a friend in
a changing room asking if the
jumpsuit is splitting a most
valuable asset apart, keep your
eyes up, take a deep breath, and
blame the designer.

FACT:
A CAMEL'S HUMP IS FULL OF FAT AND WILL
SHRINK IF THE CAMEL DOESN'T EAT.
THE SAME DOES NOT APPLY TO THE CAMEL TOE.

FASCINATING BEHAVIOR

Unlike some people,
spring for me
is not all about
racing. Not because
I don't appreciate
a bet and a nice
flute of bubbly,
but because people
seem to behave so
badly at the races.
For reasons beyond
my comprehension,
during the Kentucky
Derby it is deemed
acceptable to
start on the
cheap sparkling
at nine a.m. and
wear far too few
clothes in so-so
spring weather
or, alternatively,
acquire lobster-red
sunburn — a symptom
of being totally
moronic and maggoted
at the same time.
All this before
passing out under
a pile of coats
somewhere. Oh, and
let's not forget the
obsession with the
hats. A stupid bit
of fashion if ever
I saw one — the one
blessing being that
you can only see one
bleary eye of the
sauced-up redneck
wearing it.

UNIHEMISPHERIC SLOW-WAVE SLEEP (USWS):
WHEN ONE HALF OF AN ANIMAL'S BRAIN
SLEEPS WHILE THE OTHER HALF STAYS
ALERT. COMMONLY FOUND IN BIRDS,
DOLPHINS, SEALS, AND REDNECKS.

DÉJÀ SHOE

While trawling through a thrift
shop recently I overheard
the following conversation:

WHAT GOES AROUND

I'm a big believer in karma.
Not necessarily the kind that
says 'if you're bad you'll come
back as a slug,' more the kind
that states 'if you give away
hideous clothes on a swapping
website, you'll forever end
up with a toilet-paper tail.'
Although the idea of swapping
clothes with a complete
stranger sounds enticing, it's
also dangerous. Think about
it — how many clothes do you
actually own that you'd happily
give away? Unwanted clothes
carry a bad karma that can be
transferred between owners
as easily as syphilis. Do you
really think anyone wants a
denim wedding dress? Or a pink
ostrich-leather jacket? There
should be a rule that says you
can only swap things that you'd
happily wear yourself, but for
some reason are unable to.
Excuses I deem acceptable
would be: surprise pregnancy
to denim-clad rock star,
or loss of limbs after ostrich
attack. You get the idea.

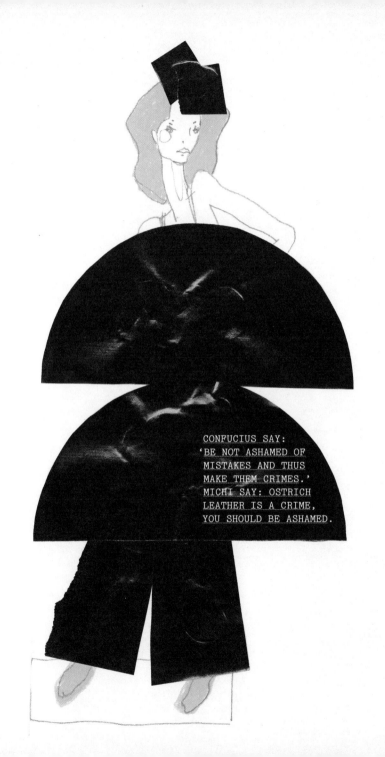

CONFUCIUS SAY:
'BE NOT ASHAMED OF
MISTAKES AND THUS
MAKE THEM CRIMES.'
MICHI SAY: OSTRICH
LEATHER IS A CRIME,
YOU SHOULD BE ASHAMED.

BRANCHING OUT

Don't get me wrong — I love a singing
whale as much as the next person.
It's just that when I first came
across organic clothes I thought
it was a bit of a scam. A bit like
that email going around about bonsai
kittens. You know, those tiny cats
in Japan that are kept in jars so
they never grow to more than just a
few centimeters long? Anyway, rather
than start another dodgy rumor about
something that doesn't exist (like
that farm in Greenland that breeds
free-range T-shirts that are all
allowed to run around and do as they
please) I thought I'd share with you
a few tips on turning your wardrobe
a nice shade of green.

1. Choose labels that use organically
certified cotton rather than rape-
and-pillage cotton. This means it is
grown in the wild and runs through the
fields with soft backlighting and a
soundtrack of modern classical music.

2. If you decide you really must wear
PVC pants, try and say no to the
plastic shopping bag that comes with it.

3. Look for anything containing hemp.
Hemp crops require no herbicides or
artificial fertilizers and not much more
than a bong full of water. For more
information, speak to your dealer.

4. Sure, it looks dodgy in furniture,
but bamboo is actually a great
substitute for artificial fibers.
And according to my friend Pixiu, the
amazing talking panda, it also tastes
delicious and makes a good weapon
for chasing away the aforementioned
rapists and pillagers.

COLOUR 'I'

GROWING ENOUGH COTTON FOR ONE T-SHIRT REQUIRES 973 LITERS OF WATER.
THAT'S A LOT OF EVIAN.

STOP
DENIM
EXPERIME
NOW !

THE SILENT VICTIMS

It seems innocent enough.
A bit of bleaching here,
a little Bedazzling there.
It's all a bit of fun, right?
Wrong. Every year, millions of
pairs of innocent denim jeans
are subjected to careless
experiments. Experiments that
are not only cruel to the
denim, but also dangerous
to anyone who inadvertently
catches a glimpse of these
hideous creations. I recently
got violently ill after
accidentally trying on a
pair of decorative rhinestone
jeans. Serves me right for
drinking and shopping.

HAVE YOU SEEN A DENIM
CRIME IN YOUR AREA?
CALL CRIMESTOPPERS
AND HELP BRING JUSTICE
BACK TO OUR STREETS.

SOME DOWN AND A PONYTAIL

Most people have quite vicious ways
of getting back at ex-boyfriends —
fish sauce in the air-con, spreading
lies on MySpace about his dirty
little porn habit, sleeping with his
friends. I would never do anything
so devious, but then my ex-boyfriend
is so easy to annoy I don't need to.
All I need to do is wear the front
of my hair up and you'd think I was
telling his mother he had crabs.
Nothing annoys a boy more than
'some down and a ponytail.' Some
other hairdos to drive men to dump:

The modern up-do

Look like you just stepped out of
bed so completely that it took a
$150-an-hour hairstylist to create
these tousled locks. Demented.

The demure headband

Every now and again the fashion set
brings it back, usually when things
have been getting out of hand and
someone decides they need to rein
in their reputation as a slut
(not to sound clichéd but often it's
Paris Hilton*). If the headband
could talk it would say 'please
don't make me do this, I feel like
I am enabling your hypocrisy.'

The high pony

Picture this — blonde, bouncy,
effervescent, high pony. You know
her, don't you? She's everyone's
friend, the nurse/physio/
occupational therapist/fill in your
preferred health professional
here ---------------------------

*<u>NOTE TO LAWYERS</u>:
<u>GOOGLE IMAGE SEARCH 'PARIS HILTON WEARING HEADBAND' = 6,950 HITS</u>
<u>GOOGLE IMAGE SEARCH 'PARIS HILTON MISADVENTURES' = 6,100 HITS</u>
<u>SPOOKILY CLOSE. COINCIDENCE? I THINK NOT</u>.

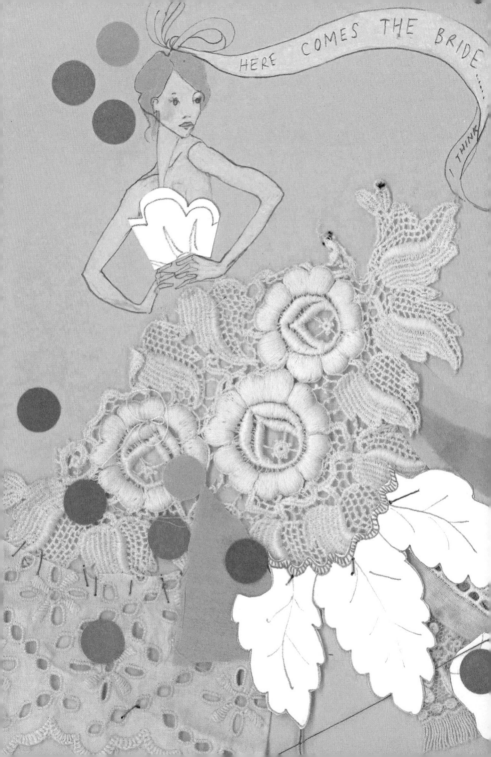

HERE COMES THE BRIDE

I THINK

HERE COMES THE BRIDE.
I THINK.

There is a golden rule
that says one should never
wear white to a wedding,
for one may be mistaken
for the bride. I would have
thought that having the
groom as an accessory was
a dead giveaway.

SCIENTIFIC FACT:
EVERYONE WEARS THEIR BEST
KNICKERS TO A WEDDING.
CLEARLY WE'RE ALL
THINKING THE SAME THING.

NEVER DATE A
GUY WHO WEARS A
LEATHER JACKET.
UNLESS OF COURSE
HE'S THE FONZ.

MAD COW DISEASE

For some reason all rules go out the
window when you're on holiday. You can
drink wine before lunch, eat chocolate
croissants without feeling guilty, you
can even get away with wearing (or not
wearing) certain clothes you'd never get
away with back home. (Depending of course
on how many croissants you've stuffed
down your pants.) On a trip to Florence,
I had one goal in mind: pick up some nice,
simple leather gloves. My friend had
given me the name of a little shop that
apparently had the 'most amazing gloves
in all of Italy.' Anyway, after hours of
walking the streets and trying to figure
out which way the map went, I finally
found the shop. And, to my surprise,
it was actually quite good. Not only
did it have lots of nice leather gloves
to choose from, it also had every other
conceivable piece of cow fashion I'd ever
seen. It was like I'd died and gone to
Suzi Quatro heaven. But in this version
of heaven, God was actually a sinewy old
woman with dyed black hair pulled into
a tight ponytail who liked to describe
everything in the shop as 'very fashion.'
'Those gloves are very fashion.' 'Yes, that
jacket is very fashion.' But it wasn't
until I picked up a pair of leather
shorts that her nonchalant expression
changed and said, 'those shorts . . .
very, very fashion.' Maybe it was the
intoxicating smell of all the leather,
or the few glasses of wine I'd had with
lunch, or maybe the sales assistant was
really a voodoo witchdoctor who liked
to put leather spells on unsuspecting
tourists. Whatever it was, it worked,
because moments later I was the proud
owner of a pair of tiny leather shorts.
It wasn't until I was walking down the
street later that night, squeezed into my
new purchase, that the spell finally wore
off and I caught a glimpse of myself in
a window looking 'very prostitute.'

WORK IT BABY

Career dressing can be a challenge, hence
the myriad glossy pages devoted to the art.
The silent language of work clothes can
leave you undone. Here are some things
to consider before leaving home.

Red in the boardroom?

Either you have penis envy or you used to
be a man — no one that assertive could
really be feminine, could they?

Are those pants sprayed on?

If we can see what you had for breakfast
and your bottom looks like a bag of peanuts,
they might be a frac too tight.

Do my boobs look
[insert appropriate paranoia]
in this?

If everyone can see them then yes,
I think they probably do.

Do I care?

That depends on whether or not you can
actually think and you have something useful
to say, or if you are relying entirely on
your bossy ballsiness, tight pants, and
gargantuan bosom to get you through.

My grandmother always said to dress for the
job you want, not the job you have. Generally
this is very sensible advice and a good rule
of thumb. Unless of course you work at the
Catholic Mission help-desk and you want to
work at the White Rhino, in which case maybe
your clothes aren't the problem.

ACCORDING TO MICHIPOLL 2008, THE MOST COMMON WORK-RELATED
FASHION MISTAKE IS EXPOSED NIPPLES. AND THAT WAS JUST ON MEN.

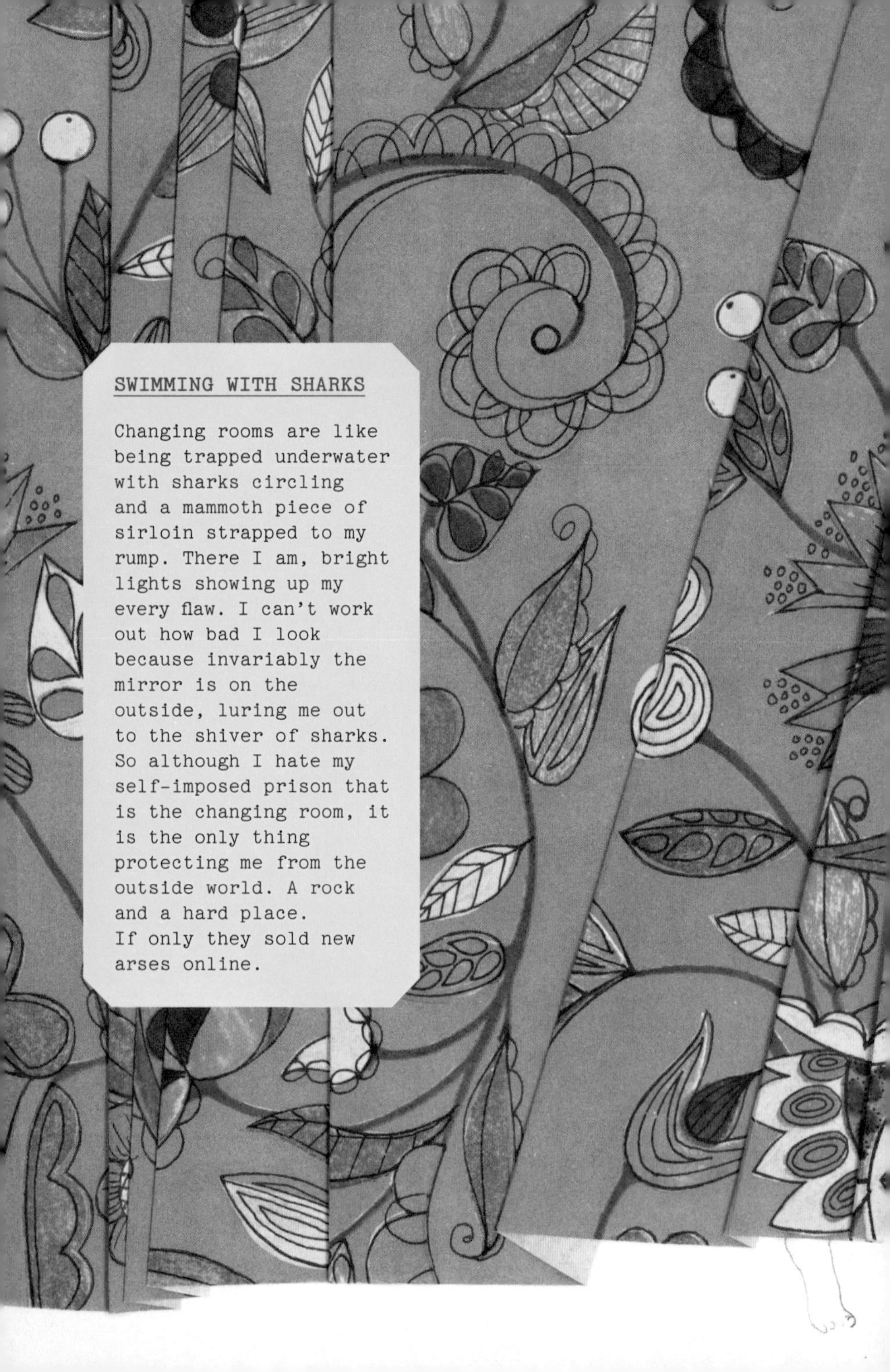

SWIMMING WITH SHARKS

Changing rooms are like
being trapped underwater
with sharks circling
and a mammoth piece of
sirloin strapped to my
rump. There I am, bright
lights showing up my
every flaw. I can't work
out how bad I look
because invariably the
mirror is on the
outside, luring me out
to the shiver of sharks.
So although I hate my
self-imposed prison that
is the changing room, it
is the only thing
protecting me from the
outside world. A rock
and a hard place.
If only they sold new
arses online.

FACT: A SHOP ASSISTANT CAN SMELL FEAR FROM TWENTY METERS AWAY.

'YOU HAVE GREAT TASTE IN BOOKS,
IT MAKES YOUR HANDS LOOK SO SLENDER' — MICHI

you clearly have such AMAZING taste...

SHOP ASSISTANCE

Note to shopkeepers:
this line works every time.

'You clearly have such
amazing taste, I just know
you will love this.'

Us mere consumers can't win —
we either admit to having bad
taste or we buy something we
actually think is ridiculous.
In return for handing you this
gem you are hereby forbidden
to use it on me.

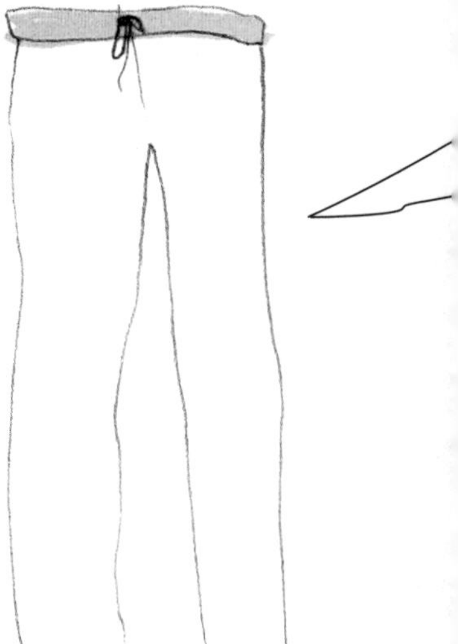

CAREER ADVICE:
UNLESS YOU ARE
MC HAMMER,
TRACKSUIT PANTS
WILL IN NO WAY
ADVANCE YOUR
CAREER STANDING.

PANTS TO THAT

I've always been confused by the term
'tracksuit.' I understand the 'track' part —
it's just the 'suit' bit that has always
thrown me. It almost implies that there
is some degree of professionalism involved
in looking like you've given up on life.
In fact, if tracksuit pants could talk
they'd probably say:

'I don't care anymore. I eat out of cans
and watch Jerry Springer.'

Of course, they'd be saying all of that
with a mouth full of synthetic sausages and
beans, so it'd be quite hard to understand,
but with the help of a translator I'm pretty
sure that's what they'd say. Anyway, it's
because of that imaginary voice in my pants
that I refuse to wear them, no matter how
warm and comfortable they claim to be. Even
on a cold winter's night I prefer to go home
to a pair of stomach-choking, thigh-strangling
jeans than don a pair of tacky pants. Call me
a snob, but I'm not quite ready to chuck in
the towel just yet.

DIET TREATMENT

(Interior, mid-afternoon, gourmet supermarket, biscuit aisle)

We see our main character, Michi, whiling away some time in the supermarket. We know it is mid-afternoon as she is adding a rather gutsy amount of chocolate biscuits to her basket — a sign she is too hungry to shop intelligently.

Pull back to wide shot (wide enough to fit her end-of-winter arse into shot)

We see she is in fact carrying two baskets of sweet treats, the kind of food that was not invented until the twentieth century, so we know she is a modern girl with expensive taste.

Michi turns the corner at the end of aisle to enter the line at the checkout. As she wobbles through she knocks over a display stand of Oreo's and pretends it was someone else. As she attempts to look nonchalant, she spies a rash of magazine covers.

ECU on magazine rack, headlines featured include:

30 days until summer! Get in shape with celebrity diets!

How Gemma Ward stays thin, tell-all diet special!

Sacrifices the stars make to look great!

Bikini countdown! Lose 20lbs before summer!

Pull out to reveal Michi's face.

A look of horror as the reality of the situation dawns on her. She comes to her senses and drops both baskets. They come crashing to the floor and we know that she has decided to throw off her old ways and embrace an active and healthy life. She strides out the exit into the sun to begin a new beginning.

Fade to black, roll credits

DIRECTOR'S CUT:

Michi earlier shoved a few packs of Oreo's up her fashionably ballooning sleeves. She takes them to the park and lies under a tree scoffing them gleefully with a large full-cream latte and British *Vogue*.

This scene was removed due to Michi being a role model to a young, potentially obese nation. Director believes the thin models in British *Vogue* easily compensate for Michi's piggery. Director stands by decision to keep this (happy) ending.

SUMMER

Tried out new fake tan. Mixed with cellulite on upper thigh makes for almost perfect ~~impersonathe~~ impersonation of a californian orange.

highest recorded
temperature ever in
the world 135°C
in Libya in
1922

- INVESTIGATE POSSIBILITY
  OF TAKING ENTIRE SEASON
  OFF WORK

- BOOK WAX — EXTRA LONG SESSION
  DUE TO SEVENTIES — LIKE 'FRO BELOW

- BOOK CAT INTO INNER - URBAN SPA
  FOR LONG WEEKEND GETAWAY

- BOOK EXTRA SHRINK APPT. FOR
  PRE AND POST HOLIDAY FAMILY
  STRESS CLEANSING.

- BEGIN INEVITABLY HOT-PINS-IN-EYES
  SEARCH FOR THE
  PERFECT BIKINI

STRING BEANS AND BIKINIS

We've all been brainwashed from an early age to believe that when it comes to swimwear, we're either a piece of meat or a piece of fruit. (Or in my case, a bag of chips and a chocolate milkshake.) But the good news is, no matter what fruit or vegetable you think you are, there's a bikini out there for you.

The apple
As my late great-grandma Granny Smith used to say, 'be proud of your appleness, show it off, but not too much—otherwise you'll end up stewing in the sun.' Try a solid one-piece with a plunging neckline for a longer appearance. Avoid boy shorts and those weird skirted bikinis. And if all that sounds like too much work, try going to a movie instead of the beach.

The
carrot

You're long
and thin and most
likely a weird
shade of orange.
But on the upside,
your long legs mean
you'll look good in
anything. Avoid vertical
stripes or you'll look
like a beanpole. And don't
wear bunny prints, as
this will only emphasize
your carrotness.

The eye fillet

You're lean and don't
have a piece of fat
on you, which means
you'll be the first
one taken by sharks in
the water. Serves you
right for being so
bloody perfect.

WHEN A PEAR
GETS TOO RIPE
IT WILL FALL
FROM THE TREE
AND GET EATEN
BY BUGS.

The pear

As a pear you want
to accentuate your positive
characteristics and draw attention away
from your less-desirable features, such as bruises
from tree branches and unsightly fruit stickers. Try pearing
(get it?) halter-style bikini tops with dark-colored high-cut
bottoms. Or better still, try some parmesan and rocket.

WARM AND STUPID

If you go through the archives of history you'll find that some of the stupidest decisions of all time have been made when it's hot and muggy. Stupid presidents are elected, hideous 4WDs are invented, ridiculous baby names are chosen, summer television programs are started, and worst of all, heat-induced fashion purchases are made. How many times have you actually used that dolphin-shaped beach bag since your last holiday? In other words, humidity leads to stupidity. Here's a chart to demonstrate my theory:

HUMIDITY   STUPIDITY

91%   Hypercolor T-shirts are invented.

93%   Jason Lee and Beth Riesgraf name
their son Pilot Inspecktor.

94%   Glenn Robinson from New Jersey patents the
technology for a mounted mechanical singing fish.

97%   A girl named Sharon gets a
dolphin tattoo on her ankle.

98%   Man invents waterproof strap for sunglasses.

99%   I have a summer fling with a guy who wears
wraparound sunglasses with a waterproof strap.
(Mind you, he was quickly dumped once the
humidity dropped.)

'LOOKS LIKE ANOTHER HUMID DAY'
— GERALD, GOLDFISH WEATHER REPORTER

IT'S NOT MANDARIN.
IT'S TANDARIN.

Now you too can have beautiful
glowing skin all year round.
Simply spray on new Tandarin
in the privacy of your own
home, and within minutes you'll
have skin just like your
favorite piece of fruit.

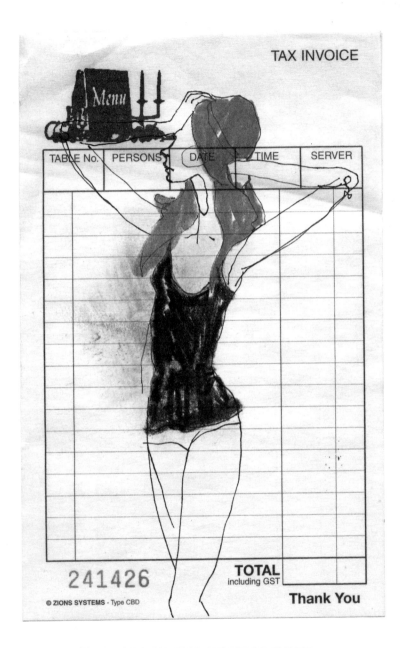

OTHER NAMES FOR THIS AFFLICTION INCLUDE
BINGO WINGS, OPRAH WINFREYS, AND TAH-TAHS.

MEAT AND GREET

There are a number of things
that come to mind in early
summer: I have nothing to wear
(again), I need a wax (again),
and I wish I didn't get my
dad's legs. My sister's list
is similar but not identical:
I have nothing to wear, I need
a wax, and I wish I didn't
have arms like a butcher.
This is a phrase that has long
puzzled me, but a sentiment I
understand. My Pilates teacher
calls them tuckshop arms.
My friends call them nana
flaps. Call them what you will,
there is a certain discomfort
in knowing that when you wave
goodbye your arm continues
waving long after your hand has
ceased. My sister finds this so
debilitating that she will not
wear tanks, strapless dresses,
or even the natty spaghetti
strap. The weird thing is, my
butcher's arms are so thin they
look like he is a vampire who
lives in a crackhouse. We may
share blood, but I'm pretty sure
we don't share cuts of meat.

Dear Michi Girl,

Just a quick note to let you know
how much I'm enjoying the book
so far. Although it's a little light on
actual fashion advice, I'm still
finding it quite useful. For example,
the other day I was out having a coffee in
the sun and realised I'd left my
sunglasses at home. But then I
realised I had a copy of your book
in my bag. It was the perfect size to
block the sun from my eyes while
I read my favourite magazine.
Keep up the good work!

Kristen

SPOT THE ADDICTION

A few years ago I developed
an insatiable appetite for
mushrooms. I don't know what
happened; it was like one day
I hated them, the next day I
couldn't get enough of them.
So much so that I ended up
baking a pie made out of five
different types of mushroom —
all of which made me so sick
I haven't been able to face
another fungus since. Now the
same thing is happening again,
but this time with spots.
Not that I'm planning to make
a pie out of spots, but I have
collected so many spotty items
that every time I open my
wardrobe it's like being back
on a mushroom trip again.

SEEING SPOTS?
THIS COULD BE CAUSED BY HIGH
BLOOD PRESSURE, A BLOW TO THE
HEAD, RETINA DAMAGE, OR YOU
COULD HAVE JUST BEEN STARING
AT THIS PAGE FOR TOO LONG.

Your waxer is male, he refers to your
pre-waxed bikini line as disco-rific,
his head has virtually disappeared
during his all-too-thorough
inspection, then he blows on
the wax. Just when you thought
it couldn't get any more
humiliating, you
find out he's
straight.

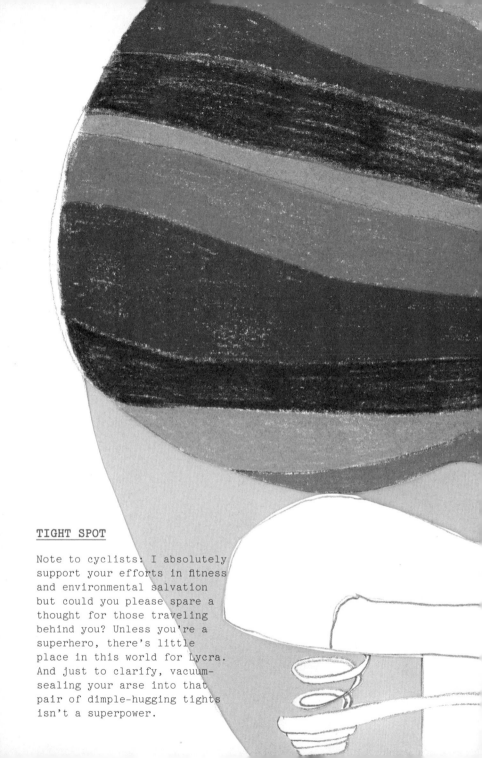

TIGHT SPOT

Note to cyclists: I absolutely
support your efforts in fitness
and environmental salvation
but could you please spare a
thought for those traveling
behind you? Unless you're a
superhero, there's little
place in this world for Lycra.
And just to clarify, vacuum-
sealing your arse into that
pair of dimple-hugging tights
isn't a superpower.

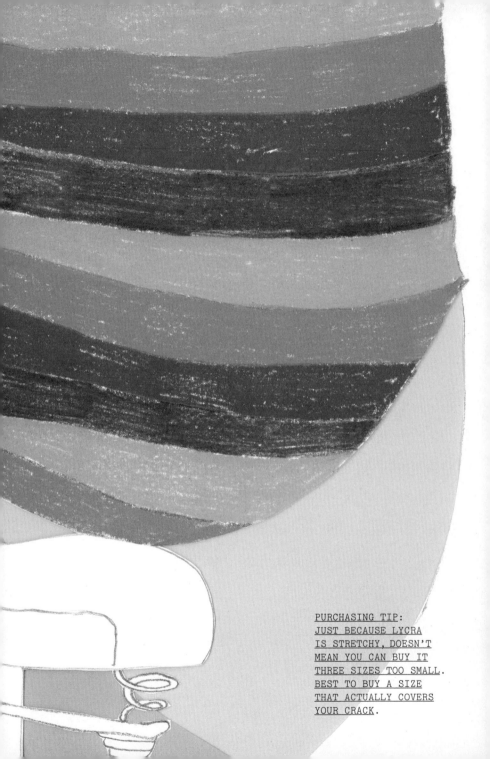

PURCHASING TIP:
JUST BECAUSE LYCRA
IS STRETCHY, DOESN'T
MEAN YOU CAN BUY IT
THREE SIZES TOO SMALL.
BEST TO BUY A SIZE
THAT ACTUALLY COVERS
YOUR CRACK.

LOW BLOW

With every evil invention comes
an equally evil by-product.

Nuclear weapon = Nuclear fallout.
Russell Crowe actor = Russell Crowe singer.
Krispy Kreme doughnut = Krispy Kreme thighs.
Low-cut hipster jeans = Lower-back tattoo.

Just like nuclear fallout, the lower-back tatt (or 'tramp stamp'
as it's so eloquently referred to) has infiltrated our society
to the point of no return, leaving hideously deformed victims
around every corner. Everywhere I look these days I'm confronted
with dragons, bats, and butterflies . . . all of which appear
to be either entering or escaping some type of cave. Recently,
while shopping at my local supermarket, I spotted a mother and
daughter team sporting matching stamps. Mum was bending over for
some sour cream while daughter was, ironically, getting some ham.

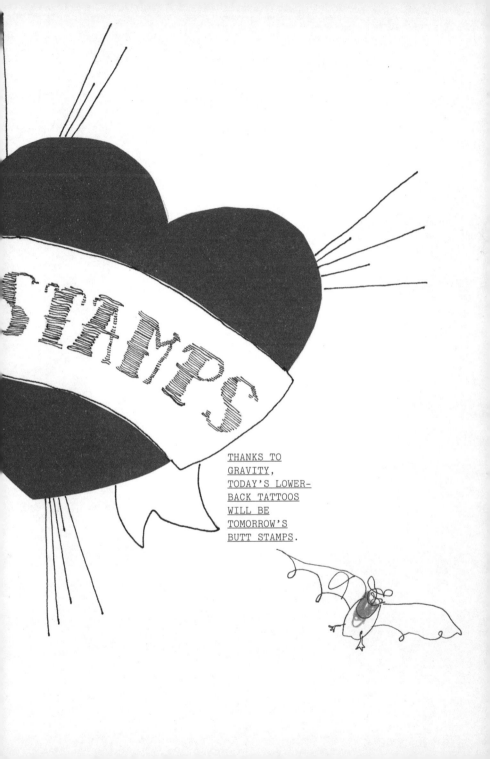

STAMPS

THANKS TO GRAVITY, TODAY'S LOWER-BACK TATTOOS WILL BE TOMORROW'S BUTT STAMPS.

YOU'VE GOTH TO BE KIDDING

Just like snow in summer
that melts into the sea
My face that was so flawless
is now sliding right off me

I long to keep my cape on
but look at the degrees!
I think I'll stay inside
with Siouxsie and her Banshees

I always thought it would be cool
to be a devil bunny
But no one warned me of this heat
now it's not so funny

I have two choices now
as far as I can tell
It's lose the Goth within me
or move further from this hell

Message to Michi — Inbox

Delete Junk Reply Reply All Forward Print

From: YourMother@michigirl.com.au
Subject: Manners
Date: 18 February 2008 5:24:45 PM
To: Michi

Dear Michi darling,

How are you today? I read the newspaper today and saw that you wrote 'shit for brains' in your column. Don't you think you could have said something a little more ladylike and less sweary? Like silly sausage? Ning nong? Your grandmother reads it, you know.

And while I'm on the subject of your column, don't make fun of people with facial hair, darling. Maybe they can't help it. Those in glass houses and all that. You never know, one day you might wake up with a random long hair growing out of your chin and then by the time you're my age you could look like Yu Zhenhuan. Then who'll be laughing?

That's all. Love and kisses,

Ma

xxx

NING NONG

NING NONG
NING NONG

NING NONG
NING NONG
NING NONG
NING NONG
NING NONG
NING NONG

0.37% of all traffic accidents are caused by people removing chin hairs at traffic lights.

WHAT'S UP YOUR BUM?

In between a hectic schedule of cave diving and
cheek flossing I caught up with the infamous Ms. G String
for this exclusive interview.

M: Firstly, would you prefer 'G' or 'Miss String'?

G: G's fine.

M: So G, what have you been up to recently?
Apart from bum cracks that is.

G: I'm sorry, what did you say?

M: I just wanted to know what you've been up to.

G: No, after that, you said something about bum cracks.

M: No I didn't.

G: Listen here Mini, or whatever your name is, if it
weren't for me, millions of women around the world would
have visible panty lines. So please, a little respect.

M: You're right, I'm sorry. No more wisecracks, I promise.

G: You just said that word again.

M: What, 'cracks'? It's just an expression.
It sounds to me that you're a little strung out.

G: Well it sounded like a pun to me.

M: Ok, I'm sorry. I promise not to make
any more bums. I mean puns.

G: I haven't got time for this shit!

M: I thought you'd be used to it by now.

G: What did you say?

M: Nothing. (Crack addict.)

G: This interview's over.

WHAT'S UP YOUR BUM?

POSITIONS VACANT: G-STRING
MUST BE WILLING TO WORK IN
TIGHT SPACES. IDEAL FIRST
JOB FOR THOSE PREPARED TO
WORK FROM THE BOTTOM UP.

NATURAL BORN HEELER

I've got a friend who does everything in heels. And I'm not
just talking about going down to the milk bar on Sunday morning
kind of everything. I'm talking let's host a BBQ wearing nothing
but a bikini and six inches of steel heel. I'm not sure why she
does it, or how she gets away with it. But she does. I, on the
other hand, can't wear anything higher than, well, my own flat
feet. The last time I tried to wear a pair of heels I got my
foot stuck in a crack in the footpath. Not only did it ruin a
beautiful pair of Marc Jacobs, it also resulted in a sprained
ankle. And if that wasn't tragic enough, it happened a few days
before going on holiday to Paris. Although my ankle eventually
heeled, the photos of me looking like le limping loser in a pair
of sneakers and a sundress will never fade.

The 'I'm your dancer for money' stiletto

Do you really need all that extra height if you're already dancing on a table? *Pronounced 'still-ett-ho'*

<u>Le French heel</u>

Named after the pint-sized King Louis XIV of France, the French heel was developed to help him get over his small-man syndrome. Clearly he had no problem with cross-dressing though.

The 'I can't be bothered' slides

The shoe equivalent of sitting on the couch and not changing the channel because you can't find the remote. Clearly my shoe of choice.

The 'look everyone, I'm crazy' clogs

Attention people of the Netherlands: please refrain from making shoes while smoking joints.

The 'Daddy, I want to be a ballerina' flats

So you always wanted to be a ballerina, but didn't make
the grade? (It's okay, neither did I.) But that doesn't mean
you can't play the part. First it was the tiara, now you
want the slippers. What's next — a pony?

FORMER FIRST LADY OF THE PHILIPPINES IMELDA MARCOS WAS BELIEVED TO HAVE
1,060 PAIRS OF SHOES. BUT MORE IMPRESSIVELY, HALLE BERRY IS RUMORED
TO HAVE SIX TOES. (SERIOUSLY, GOOGLE IT IF YOU DON'T BELIEVE ME.)

NEVER TRUST A MAN
IN MOHAIR TRUNKS.

THE INVISIBLE LINE

If you're reading this
while sitting in a
suburban cafe wearing
nothing but a bikini,
chances are you've
crossed it. 'It'
being the invisible
line where swimwear
becomes underpants.
Some people think the
line ends where the
sand does. Other
people are a bit more
lax with the rules and
think it's okay as long
as you can still see
the water. I, on the
other hand, prefer to
use a sliding scale
to determine how far
you can travel from
the beach in swimwear
before it becomes,
well, wrong. For example,
if you're a hairy,
middle-aged man wearing
beige budgie smugglers,
then the line is your
towel and not an inch
further — no strolls,
no chatting by the
shore, preferably no
swimming. However, on
the other end of my
flexi-scale, if you're
Jude Law then the line
is more like an arc.
By all means, Jude
look-alike, take a walk,
go for coffee, hell,
you can even catch a
bus for all I care.
In fact why not turn
the invisible line
into invisible trunks?

You never saw a barnacle's winkle at noon.

it takes about one million cloud droplets to provide enough water for one raindrop.

AUTUMN

Bought second-hand boots under the impression they once belonged to Bianca Jagger. Turns out they were corn-inducing and probably something bad and probably belonged to Pam Ayers.

Vintage my arse.

Op shop now.

- THINK ABOUT WHY BEARS DO WHAT THEY DO, AND SEE IF ANY POSSIBILITY OF HUMANS GETTING ANY OF THAT SWEET HIBERNATING ACTION.

- CALL SHRINK RE ONSET OF UNUSUAL SENSE OF WELL BEING. POSSIBLE REASONS — NO LONGER BEING XRAYED EVERY TIME I WALK OUTSIDE INTO SUNSHINE OR MAY BE DUE TO FIRST DROP OF WINTER INSTORE? EITHER WAY, HARD TO TRUST OVERWHELMING HAPPINESS I SHOULD BE ADDRESSED.

- CALL MUM ABOUT PRUNING — HAVE A FEELING IT IS TIME TO DO SOMETHING IN THE GARDEN BUT CAN'T REMEMBER WHAT IT IS.

TWO FOR THE PRICE OF ONE

When I was in kindergarten I wanted to wear everything I could find.
It's a common preschooler thing, I believe. But then I grew up.
I developed the ability to decide whether to wear a skirt or pants.
I am an adult. But apparently some of you still can't decide,
hence the interesting Siamese development known as the skouser.
Can't decide between skirt or trousers? Want to wear a skirt but
your legs are too hairy? Love pants but you think your bum is too
fat? No problem. Pop a skirt over the top or, better still, buy a
skouser. Bit hot? Then the skort is for you — shorts with a skirt
over the top. Perfect. Just like a baby wearing a diaper.
You must be so proud.

SKOUSER

SARCASM IS THE LOWEST
FORM OF WIT AND THE
MOST EFFECTIVE.
SKOUSERS ARE THE LOWEST
FORM OF GARMENT AND THE
LEAST ATTRACTIVE.

THOMAS BURBERRY
INVENTED THE TRENCH
COAT FOR SOLDIERS
IN 1901. IT'S NOW
2008 AND I'M A WOMAN
— NEED I SAY MORE?

ENTRENCHED

Fashion editors love to bang on about
the importance of the classic trench coat.
I don't get it. I understand it was a
must for the man in the Botanic Gardens
who wanted to urgently show me something
behind a rotunda last year. I also
understand it is useful for those many
occasions when you absolutely must get
somewhere on public transport in black
lacy smalls. I can even kind of get it
for the odd occasion when you need to
sneak an AK-47 into the office. But, let's
face it. Unless you're a flashing hooker
with an assault rifle catching the tram
to a party dressed up as Lancelot Link
Secret Chimp, won't a raincoat do?

to the
— BE
TYPES

JUST BECAUSE CUSTOMIZING BECAME
FASHIONABLE, IT DOESN'T MAKE YOU
A FASHION DESIGNER. IF IT DID
THEN I WOULD HAVE HAD A NEW
CAREER THE DAY I DISCOVERED
THE BEDAZZLER. LET'S EVERYONE
TRY TO LEAVE T-SHIRT PRINTS TO
THE PROFESSIONALS, SHALL WE?

FISHING FOR THE TRUTH

Can't decide whether it's appropriate to wear fishnets to work? Fill out this conclusive five-step survey to find out the answer to one of life's most enduring questions: 'Does wearing fishnets to work make me a stripper?'

1. When you get paid, your money goes into:

A. An online bank account
B. A brown paper bag
C. A garter belt

2. You spend most of your day behind:

A. A computer
B. A work bench
C. A pole

3. Your boss's name is:

A. Sally
B. Bernard
C. Jake the Snake

4. The song that best describes your career is:

A. '9 to 5' — Dolly Parton
B. 'Working on the Highway' — Bruce Springsteen
C. 'Private Dancer' — Tina Turner

5. The first thing you do when someone around you gets sick is:

A. Call the doctor
B. Administer first aid
C. Put on a saucy nurse's uniform

RESULTS:

A = 1 point
B = 2 points
C = 5 points

5–8 points:

I'm sorry to say this but you work in an office, which means fishnets are probably not going to advance your career. Unless of course you want to work on top of the desk instead of behind it.

9–14 points:

You're a male construction worker, which means you shouldn't be wearing fishnets or even reading this book, for that matter.

15 points and over:

Congratulations, you're either an exotic dancer or a transvestite in a popular stage show. Either way, you can wear your fishnets to work with confidence.

to blouse. *verb.* The act of
trying on clothes that you
have absolutely no intention
(or means) of purchasing;
'I'd love to purchase this
beautiful Miu Miu top but
unfortunately I left my purse
in my car, which is currently
on my boat. So today I'm just
blousing thank you.'

SEE ALSO 'SHOP LOBSTER':
'MAY I HELP YOU, OR ARE YOU
JUST HAPPY GETTING YOUR
CLAWS ALL OVER OUR CLOTHES
LIKE A SHOP LOBSTER?'

QUESTIONS & ARSES

Recent studies show that
the average woman spends
nearly four years of her
life worrying about her
weight. Not only is this
an unhealthy practice,
it's also a complete
waste of time as you need
at least eight years of
stress to burn some serious
calories. So to help stay
in shape all year round,
I aim to spend at least
an hour a day trying to
work out the following:

Why do people
wear earrings
to the beach?
(3 x sets of 10)

If they didn't print
the words 'do not eat'
on those little sachets
inside shoeboxes,
would people really
try and eat them?
(5 minute warm-up)

Why tie-dye?
(4 x sets of 8)

What exactly is
haberdashery?
(Hold for 2 minutes)

Who decided that we
needed buckles on shoes?
(3 x sets of 10)

60-YEAR
MONEY BACK
GUARANTEE!

Does anyone ever use
those stupid little
pockets on the front
of jeans?
(3 x sets of 12)

IF YOU DO NOT EXPERIENCE
SUBSTANTIAL WEIGHT LOSS AFTER
SIXTY YEARS OF USING THESE
CALORIE-BURNING QUESTIONS YOU
MAY BE ELIGIBLE FOR A FULL OR
PARTIAL REFUND OF THIS BOOK.

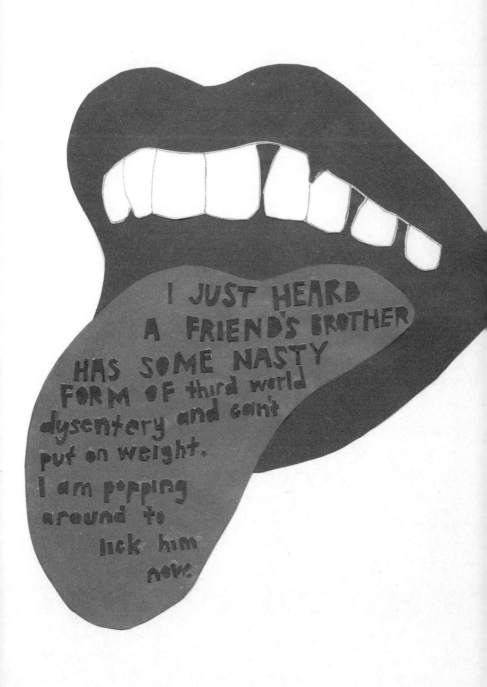

MY MOTHER
ALWAYS SAID
'STAND OVER
THE SEAT OF
A PUBLIC TOILET.'
PERHAPS FOR
MRS. PANAYIOTOU-
MICHAEL SOMETHING
WAS LOST IN
TRANSLATION
AND LITTLE GEORGE
THOUGHT SHE SAID
'ALWAYS BEND OVER
THE TOILET SEAT.'

CHOOSE LIFE
(AND GET OVER IT)

When George Michael wore
a Katharine Hamnett 'Choose
Life' T-shirt, I reckon he
meant choose your own life
rather than regurgitate
someone else's bad taste.
Or did I miss something?
Did they really mean
choose the 80s – again?
Gold spandex and fluoro
headbands, asymmetrical
haircuts and acid washes
– do we have to? Enough
with the freakin' 80s
revivals already. Since
when was George Michael
a role model anyway?
If we all followed him
we'd be in the toilet
(publicly), wouldn't we?

A DIP IN THE JEAN POOL

Depending on the gene pool you've crawled out of, shopping for a new pair of denim pins can be one of life's most painful experiences. Clearly I come from quite a shallow gene pool that likes to compare jean shopping with childbirth, amputation, and being born with an angry conjoined twin on your shoulder that can only communicate by biting you on the neck. In other words, I find the whole thing a little irritating. So when I do finally find a pair that does fit, I welcome them into my wardrobe like a member of the family. Speaking of which, my last pair of jeans ended up on the adoption pile after biting me on the stomach. Either they were too tight or just trying to tell me they loved me. If it was the latter, I'm terribly sorry.

'HEY, NO RUNNING!' — GENE POOL LIFEGUARD

OH DEER, THERE ARE
CURRENTLY OVER 1.5 MILLION
WEB PAGES THAT FEATURE OR
REFERENCE A DEER BROOCH.

FASHION VERMIN

noun. a once-cute animal that has become far too popular for
its own good by infiltrating everything from T-shirts, earrings,
brooches, knickers, logos, leggings, and every other conceivable
piece of fashion fodder. Recent additions to the not-so-endangered
species list include bluebirds, owls, squirrels, bunnies, and most
common of all, the deer. 'Fawnicate me, that's the tenth deer brooch
I've seen this week! The poor thing's become fashion vermin.'

BLOODY MARYS AND BOOKS DON'T MIX

<u>ALL THOSE IN FAVOR, RAISE A LEG</u>

SIGN THE PAWS PETITION AND PUT AN END TO BADLY DRESSED PETS

Dear President / Prime Minister / King / Queen
(insert appropriate dignitary)

Every second of every day, an innocent pet becomes the victim
of some form of fashion cruelty. Puffy jackets on Portuguese
Pointers, terry cloth trench coats on Toy Fox Terriers, sequined
singlets on Shih Tzus, mini-skirts on Münsterländers; these are
just some of the horrific wardrobe malfunctions that
I have spotted walking past my house in the last few seconds.
And we call (insert country) a civilized country?

I for one have had enough and have decided to join PAWS
(Pets Against Wardrobe malfunctions) — a not-for-profit
organization set up by our fearless leader Michi Girl. Through
the kindness of her own heart, Michi has asked me to ask you
to get behind our cause and put an end to badly dressed pets
for good. And in the process, maybe even nominate her for some
kind of humanitarian award that comes with a cash prize.

We may not be able to stop (insert badly dressed celebrity) from
dressing like a dog, but surely we can stop dogs from dressing
like (insert previously mentioned badly dressed celebrity).

Yours in good taste,

The Undersigned

'IF I HAD OPPOSABLE THUMBS I'D SIGN THE OFFICIAL PAWS PETITION AT
WWW.THEPETITIONSITE.COM/PETITION/118389666'
                              - SCOOTER, STOCKHOLM, SWEDEN

NO ONE
LOOKS
GOOD IN
MUSTARD.
UNLESS OF COURSE
YOU'RE A HOT DOG.

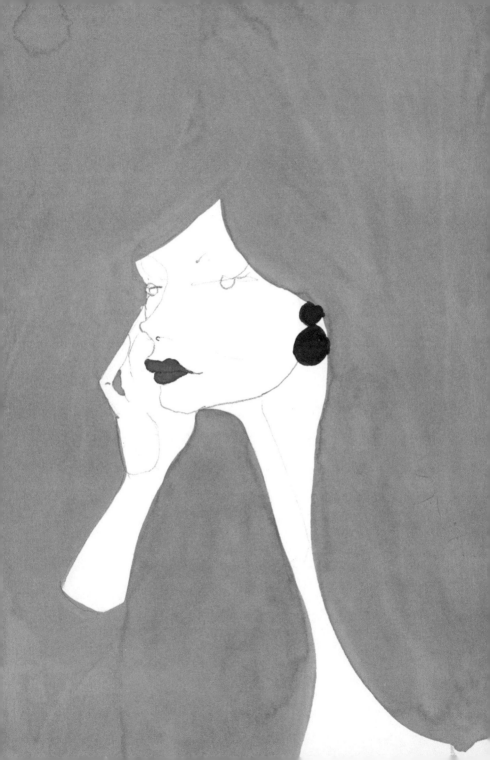

NO LOOKING BACK

As hard as it is to believe, looking the way I do, I avoid
mirrors like the plague. I have a small mirror in my bathroom
that is useful for the shoulder-up view, but a big mirror is
something I just couldn't entertain. Some people won't leave
the house without a good old once-over. Me, I prefer visual
ignorance and rely heavily on my friends' brutal honesty.
No one in their right mind wants to know that they look like
Mrs. Doubtfire from behind. Why spoil a perfectly good morning
by having to refer to an animal book to identify the beast
you see before you?

FACT: AN ADULT
CHIMPANZEE
WILL NOT ALWAYS
RECOGNIZE ITS OWN
REFLECTION WHEN
GIVEN A MIRROR.

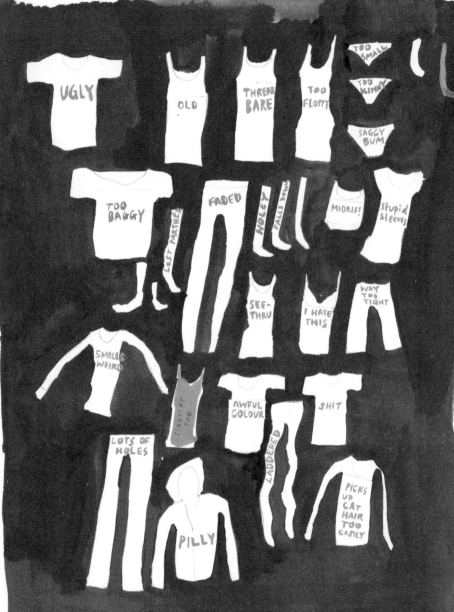

SWEAT SHOPPING

In my wardrobe, exercise clothes have always been the items that didn't make the cut in my day-to-day wear. Ugly T-shirts, old tights, orphan socks — pretty much the same thing I wear to paint the house. The theory being that the more hideous I look, the less time I'll want to spend in public looking like a blotchy baboon's ass. Therefore dramatically reducing my exercise regime and giving me more time to sit in front of the television and laugh at people trying to exercise on reality-based weight-loss shows. It's a win-win.

IT IS PROVEN THAT YOU WILL RUN 20% FASTER IN A PAISLEY LYCRA BODY SUIT.

CANKLES TO BOOT

My best friend waits every year for
autumn. The season's first delivery of
long boots is on her radar like a free
Marni coat is on mine. And each year
is the same — ankles snipped in zips,
calves pouring over the top like a
muffin. And each year the question:
'Do you think loose boots will be back
in this year? It's very *Flashdance* but
I am okay with that.' Fat calves and
ankles (or cankles if you will) are
one thing no amount of nips and tucks
can help. You can be the most perfect
specimen but never find a knee-high
boot that will zip up, therefore
closing the door on many a good skirt.
Fat-ankled girls just go straight
from knee to foot without the segue
that the rest of us enjoy, that subtle
transition from one to the other.
It's like two lanes converging to one
without the dotted line — confusing
and weird to look at. Like a rugby
player upside down, it's just a bit
wrong. Poor love, she's condemned to
pants forever. Or leg warmers.

CANKLE FORMULA:
C = K < A
KEY:
C = CANKLE
K = KNEE
A = ANKLE

WINTER

- RESEARCH SNAILS - HEARD THEY CAN SLEEP FOR THREE YEARS. MAYBE BETTER OPTION THAN HIBERNATING BEAR ENVY.

- BOOK FACIAL - REMEMBER TO ASK ABOUT PERPETUALLY DARK RINGS UNDER EYES. PERHAPS THERE IS SOME WAY TO MICHAEL JACKSON THEM OUT?

- BOOK EXTRA SHRINK APPTS TO DISCUSS ANOTHER FINANCIAL YEAR COMING AROUND WITHOUT A HOUSE DEPOSIT BEING SAVED. SEIZURE.

- THINK ABOUT WHETHER MENTALLY STRONG ENOUGH TO GO JEANS SHOPPING WHILE SOBER.

decided to dye hair a nice chocolate brown for winter.

the coupling of hair and cement coloured face makes me look like a Wink ice-cream. I hope no one licks me accidentally

On July 4, 1956 in Maryland USA, over 3cm of rain fell in just one minute

it is said that in 1983 it got as cold as -89.6°C in Vostok Station, Antartica – without windchill.

IF YOU DIDN'T
PAY FOR THIS BOOK,
CHANCES ARE YOU'RE
WEARING A HOODIE.

PUTTING THE HOOD BACK IN HOODLUM

Gone are the good old days when wearing a hoodie meant you were
either a petty crim or some kind of underworld figure. Now it
appears that everywhere I look people are jumping onto the hooded
bandwagon. Over recent years kids, mums, nerds, pet dogs, and even
monks have turned the humble hoodie into a ubiquitous piece of
fashion attire. (Okay, I take that last bit back about the monks
— apparently they've been wearing hoodies since the Middle Ages.)
But the point is, the hoodlum has well and truly been taken out
of the hoodie. Recently I even purchased a ridiculously expensive
silk and cashmere hoodie — which of course cost so much I was
forced to steal food for the next week to pay for it.

RAINING CATS AND FROGS

Over the centuries there have
been thousands, maybe even
dozens, of sightings of weird
things falling from the sky.
Fish rain, frog rain, 'gator
rain, squid rain, and worm rain
are just some of the strange
rains that have been periodically
reported around the world.
But what hasn't been documented
(until now of course) are the
equally strange umbrellas people
use to protect themselves from
such unseasonal rainfall.

Tombrella

What Katie Holmes should have
used to protect herself from the
oncoming Scientology wet patch.

Numbrella

The beach umbrella that gets
swept away by the wind and stabs
you in the neck, making you numb
from the waist down.

Thumbrella

The cocktail umbrella used by
tiny people such as Tom Thumb
and Tom Cruise when it rains.

Ummbrella

The umbrella you can never find
when you need it. 'Umm, has anyone
seen my ummbrella? I'm sure I
left it, um, here last week.'

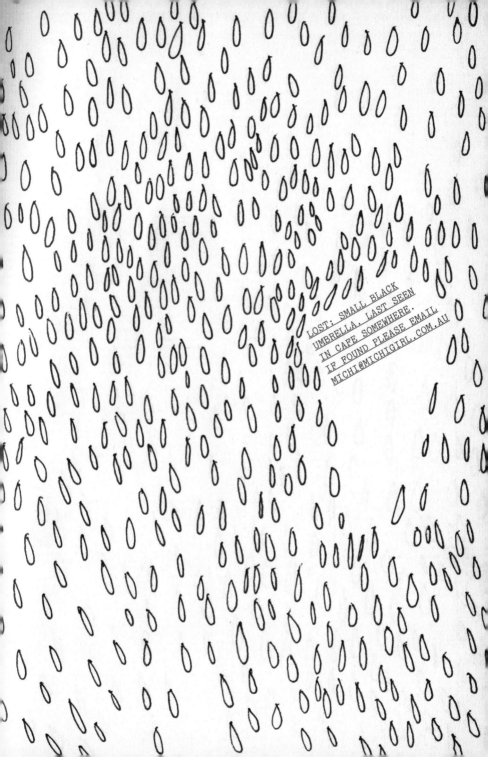

LOST: SMALL BLACK
UMBRELLA. LAST SEEN
IN CAFE SOMEWHERE.
IF FOUND PLEASE EMAIL
MICHI@MICHIGIRL.COM.AU

SOMETIMES I WISH
I COULD LABEL MYSELF
'HAND WASH ONLY'
FOR THOSE EXTRA
delicate days.

BAG LADY

Bags are taking over my life.
While packing for a holiday
recently I discovered that
I'd actually packed six
different bags. (Seven, if
you count the suitcase that
was carrying them all.)
And that was just for a
one-week holiday. At this
rate I'm destined to end
up walking the streets with
one of those giant red,
white, and blue stripy hobo
numbers. I wonder if I'll
find shoes to match?

MENTAL NOTE:
MATCHING SHOES MAY NOT
BE NUMBER ONE PRIORITY
IF LIVING ON THE
STREETS DUE TO OVER-
PURCHASING OF BAGS.

The pretty, but impractical, useless clutch

As the name suggests,
this bag is pretty
much useless. Designed
to fit a car key and
a maxed-out credit
card, the clutch is
about as useful as
having a sixth finger.

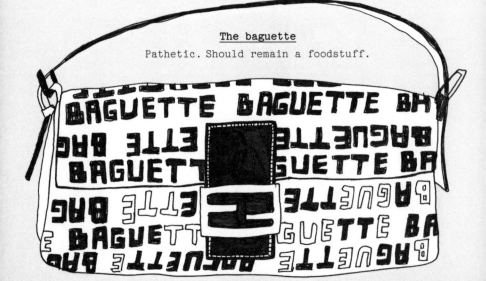

The baguette
Pathetic. Should remain a foodstuff.

The practical, but ugly, oversized tote

Killed someone and haven't got time to hide the body?
This massively awkward bag is perfect for life's misdemeanors.

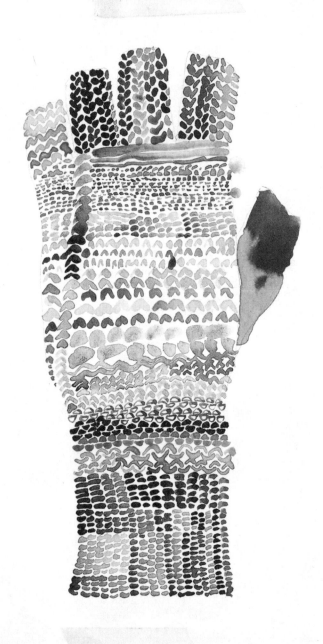

OPEN-ENDED LETTER

Dear Inventor of the Fingerless Glove,

I hope this letter finds you well. Firstly, congratulations
on your invention; it appears to be still in demand after
all these years. You must be pleased. Now, I apologize if
this sounds like a stupid question, but I'm curious as to
what the original idea behind your design was? I was always
led to believe that the sole purpose of a glove is to keep
one's hands warm — in particular one's fingers. Now, I'm not
a doctor, but I've been doing a little research of my own
and have yet to find a medical condition where someone's
hands get cold while their fingers simultaneously overheat.
Or perhaps I'm missing the point of your invention? Does it
have something to do with an ancient tribal tradition where
the fingers are considered an erogenous zone and leaving them
exposed is a form of foreplay? Sort of like Fijian women
and their ankles, but in reverse? Or is there some rare
genetic disease where the fingers swell to the size of chorizo
sausages and the fingerless glove is the only design flexible
enough to cater for their inflated phalanges?
Or did you just run out of wool?

Yours sincerely,

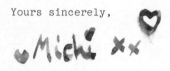

Michi xx

THE WOOL SAVED FROM
MAKING FINGERLESS GLOVES
IS OFTEN USED TO KEEP
SHEEP WARM IN WINTER.

Just as a treat, Google Image Search 'Lee Redmond' and at the same time think about the question of maintaining personal hygiene.

MANNARIES

Yesterday I sat next to a
man who had nipples larger
than a breastfeeding
mother and I could see
them through his T-shirt.
Every time I think about
it I get a little bit of
sick in my mouth.

SPAM > MAKE HORN3
WITH FAK3
NIPP!3S!!! ONLY
$3.25. CLICK
HERE FOR FREE
SHIPPING!!!

DONE TO DEATH

The way movies spawn fashion trends is something that has never quite made sense to me. I can kind of understand the way we all cuffed our jeans and wore flats when Cameron Diaz did it in *There's Something About Mary*. Who wouldn't want to look like that? I can also understand getting a bit more luxe after seeing *Marie Antoinette*. But there is a big leap from luxury to sea-shanty in the recent skull-obsessed pirate parade we witnessed. For heaven's sake. If you really want to dress like a drunken sea captain, why not just retain bed hair at all times and go on a three-day bender? Oh sorry, Whitney, you already did.

THE HAT THING

There are hats and there are hats. There are
sensible beach hats for avoiding hideous cancers.
These are acceptable, if not encouraged.
There are hats for funerals and races, which,
although usually rancid, are sometimes unavoidable.
But then there is the other kind. There is the
hat that is 'the thing.' You know, the guy who
always wears a hat because it's 'his thing.'
This kind of hat, no matter how embarrassed
he might be by his male pattern baldness,
or how cool he thinks he looks, is absolutely
and utterly ridiculous. I would be so bold as
to say that I would drop a boy like a hot chip
if he started on one of those hat jags.

The cap

The baseball cap can mean one of the following:
He is a petty thief; he carries the burden of
ridiculously low self-esteem; he has bad manners
or, quite likely, he has a weird-shaped head.
Potentially all of the above are true. In fact this
is the most likely scenario as one often leads to
another. It all starts with the weird-shaped head.

The bad beanie

Another hat favored by the petty crim is the
beanie. It is also a staple in the wardrobe of the
neo-Nazi and the ski instructor. The common trait
here is arrogance in disguise — all of them think
they know better than you but don't want you to
know that.

The not-so-bad beanie

A Rastafarian may wear a beanie filled with
dreadlocks, which is acceptable as it is a religious
belief rather than a 'thing' and even I won't hold
that against a man.

The victim

Then there is the worst kind: fashion-victim-
hat-wearer. His hat changes with the season/
the fashion/Johnny Depp's. It goes without
saying that this guy is to be avoided.
He is, quite simply, a knob.

93% OF PEOPLE WHO WEAR BASEBALL CAPS HAVE SOMETHING TO HIDE.

COMING SOON:
'ON THE NOSE' — THE OVERPOWERING
NEW FRAGRANCE BY MICHI GIRL.

STINKERS

Paris Hilton is a genius. No, really. Who else would have come up with a name for her own perfume as brilliant as hers? Paris Hilton by Paris Hilton. A gem as original as the lady herself.

And Britney's Curious. Curious about how a sweet orange-flower and fresh grapefruit combination can go from spicy schoolgirl to fermented old fruit tart overnight? Ask Britney.

How about the Beckhams? Their agents call him 'a portrait of modern masculinity' and her 'multitalented.' One would expect these his-and-her fragrances to have some staying power. Quite frankly, his is a bit thick and hers almost non-existent. Surprised?

And then there's Celine Dion. Celine is an old pro in the fragrance biz with a fourth foray into the market. It may hit the high notes and harmonize well but somehow it still manages to reek of mediocrity.

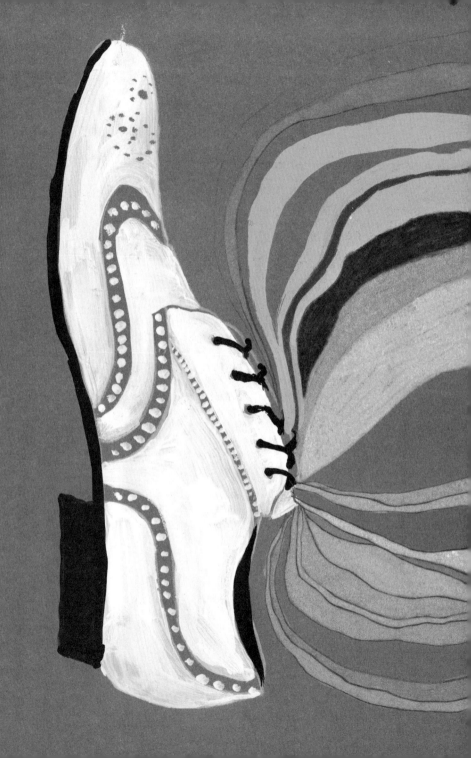

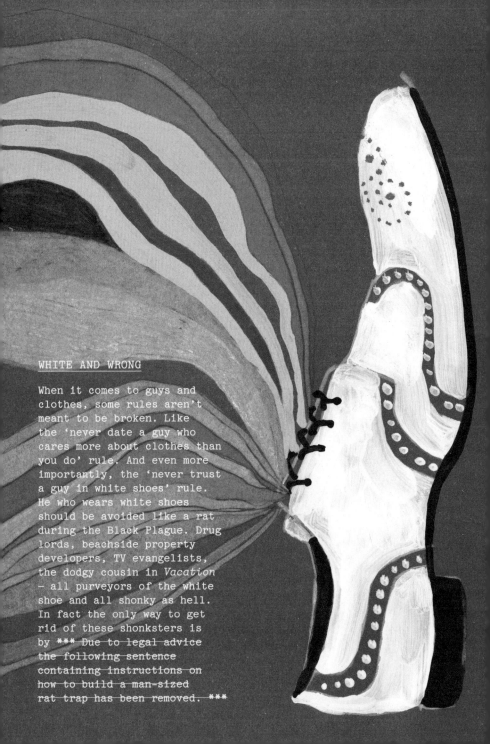

WHITE AND WRONG

When it comes to guys and clothes, some rules aren't meant to be broken. Like the 'never date a guy who cares more about clothes than you do' rule. And even more importantly, the 'never trust a guy in white shoes' rule. He who wears white shoes should be avoided like a rat during the Black Plague. Drug lords, beachside property developers, TV evangelists, the dodgy cousin in *Vacation* — all purveyors of the white shoe and all shonky as hell. In fact the only way to get rid of these shonksters is by ~~*** Due to legal advice the following sentence containing instructions on how to build a man-sized rat trap has been removed.~~ ***

REGRET NOTHING

I am happy to say that there are very few fashion purchases that I regret. I am generally quite good at buying clothes as long-term friends rather than one-night stands. (Forgetting of course that tussle in my twenties with the terribly dashing yet highly volatile and unattainable artist. Oh my.) There is one thing, however, that I do regret. I once spent an insane amount of money on a Marni skirt in New York in a mad hungover dash into Barney's on the way to JFK. I thought, 'This is mental, I should be buying something useful like that black tailored winter coat.' But I didn't. I bought a skirt that looks average on me and goes with nothing else I own, because my friend dared me to. Every time I put it on I think of the black coat I wish I owned. The moral of the story is that you shouldn't regret the things you do, you should regret the things you don't do. I don't regret the skirt (I was dared — what could I do?). I do regret not buying the posh wool coat. So next time you are thinking that you shouldn't go home with that truly exotic man that you sense is trouble (but a boon in the trouser department), or thinking that you really ought to prioritize the rent over the Louboutins, think of my (almost) black coat. Or the artist, whichever works for you. Either way, regret nothing. It's a waste of time.

POST-PURCHASE
COGNITIVE DISSONANCE:
THAT VIOLENTLY ILL
FEELING YOU HAVE
WHEN YOU HAVE BOUGHT
THE WRONG THING ON
CREDIT FOR WAY TOO
MUCH MONEY.

THE RORSCHACH TEST

Last night when I went to
bed I found that a piece of
Toblerone had slipped down
the heavenly valley and
melted into two ants, one
on each boob. I wonder if
I could make a butterfly with
the help of a push-up bra?

THERE IS A DEGREE COURSE
IN BRA STUDIES AVAILABLE
IN HONG KONG. I ASSUME
THEY ARE VERY SUPPORTIVE.

DRESS CODE CODE

Smart casual

Try to avoid denim and keep
yourself nice(ish). Get drunk
enough to seem casual, but
not so drunk that you are
no longer smart.

Formal

Rent a tux. If you want to
appear slightly more formal,
try and stay upright.

Black tie

Wear your own dinner suit. You
wouldn't be seen dead renting
a tuxedo. If you don't know the
difference, you're not invited.

Semi-formal

Borrow a cheap suit and don't
bother keeping yourself upright.

Ultra formal

I don't know what this is but
my instinct tells me it is code
for ultra redneck. I'm thinking
formal with a pre-tied, novelty
print bow-tie and a walking cane
that doubles as a hip flask.

Creative black tie

Think unbuttoned band-collars,
shoestring ties, black shirts,
and anything else that
advertising execs would
wear to an award dinner to
appear more creative.

NOT SURPRISINGLY, THE PENGUIN HAS WON MORE 'BEST DRESSED'
AWARDS THAN ANY OTHER ANIMAL.

THERE ARE 171,476
WORDS IN THE
OXFORD ENGLISH
DICTIONARY, BUT
NOTHING TO DESCRIBE
THAT ANNOYING
SWOOSHING NOISE
ONE'S THIGHS MAKE
WHILE WALKING IN
A PAIR OF CORDS.

A LITTLE TOO CORD-INATED

I used to have a boyfriend
who liked to wear cord
jeans with cord jackets.
Depending on the color
of the cord, on any given
day he either looked like
a licorice strap or a
carrot. I had to drop
him in the end. I hope he
doesn't read this book.

A BIENTOT

As winter drags on I get an
overwhelming feeling that I want
to commit a terrible crime.
Each year I am increasingly
affected by Seasonal Affective
Disorder (SAD). This year,
to avoid stealing a frock or
slashing my idiot neighbor's
tires, I have decided to curtail
my winter blues and head for
Paris. What better way to
celebrate the end of this book
but by giving you the bird and
flying away? Can you picture it?
That's me looking as sensual
as the Venus de Milo as I pass
the Musée du Louvre. I am
nonchalantly buying Eiffel Tower
glow-in-the-dark condoms like an
old pro (me, awkward? No!).
I am catching the Metro to
Saint-Paul pretending not to see
the painfully over-the-top
PDA going on at the exit.
I pop up in the Marais, like a
new spring petal ready to shop
and take on the world.

Of course in the real version
I stare at the make-out session
so obviously that I get caught
and trip, falling down two
flights of stairs into an
overflowing ashtray surrounded
by suitably do-able French men.

Quel embarras.

'DRINKING WHEN WE ARE NOT THIRSTY AND MAKING LOVE AT ALL SEASONS, MADAM: THAT IS ALL THERE IS TO DISTINGUISH US FROM OTHER ANIMALS.'

P.A. CARON DE BEAUMARCHAIS, 1732–1799

Michi would like to thank everyone at Penguin
for their blind faith. A special thank you
to Kirsten Abbott for your kind and generous
spirit and numerous deadline extensions.
Also thanks to Jess Crouch, Deb Brash and Sue
Van Velsen. Thank you to Peter Mescalchin
for putting me online all these years and
forgiving my non-existent technical prowess.
Big thanks to the extended family — mums,
dads, sisters, brothers, friends, kids and
cats, you know who you are. Super special
thanks to Scott and Gab for being so gorgeous
and encouraging and not complaining about
my tendency towards spontaneity. And lastly,
thank you to Kat and Sim for your dedication
to making me look so beautiful and for
your endless talent and love.

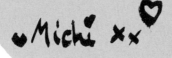